The Grub-Street opera. As it is acted at the theatre in the Hay-Market. By Scriblerus Secundus. To which is added, The masquerade, a poem. Printed in MDCCXXVIII.

Henry Fielding

ECCO
PRINT EDITIONS

The Grub-Street opera. As it is acted at the theatre in the Hay-Market. By Scriblerus Secundus. To which is added, The masquerade, a poem. Printed in MDCCXXVIII.

Fielding, Henry
ESTCID: T035895
Reproduction from British Library
Scriblerus Secundus = Henry Fielding. 'The masquerade' has a separate titlepage dated 1728; the register is continuous. 'The Welsh opera' was the first published unauthorised edition with 31 songs, 'The genuine Grub-street opera' was the second unauthor
London : printed, and sold by J. Roberts, 1731.
[8],56,[4],11,[1]p. ; 8°

ECCO
ECCO
Eighteenth Century
Collections Online
Print Editions

Gale ECCO Print Editions

Relive history with *Eighteenth Century Collections Online*, now available in print for the independent historian and collector. This series includes the most significant English-language and foreign-language works printed in Great Britain during the eighteenth century, and is organized in seven different subject areas including literature and language; medicine, science, and technology; and religion and philosophy. The collection also includes thousands of important works from the Americas.

The eighteenth century has been called "The Age of Enlightenment." It was a period of rapid advance in print culture and publishing, in world exploration, and in the rapid growth of science and technology – all of which had a profound impact on the political and cultural landscape. At the end of the century the American Revolution, French Revolution and Industrial Revolution, perhaps three of the most significant events in modern history, set in motion developments that eventually dominated world political, economic, and social life.

In a groundbreaking effort, Gale initiated a revolution of its own: digitization of epic proportions to preserve these invaluable works in the largest online archive of its kind. Contributions from major world libraries constitute over 175,000 original printed works. Scanned images of the actual pages, rather than transcriptions, recreate the works *as they first appeared.*

Now for the first time, these high-quality digital scans of original works are available via print-on-demand, making them readily accessible to libraries, students, independent scholars, and readers of all ages.

For our initial release we have created seven robust collections to form one the world's most comprehensive catalogs of 18th century works.

Initial Gale ECCO Print Editions collections include:

History and Geography
Rich in titles on English life and social history, this collection spans the world as it was known to eighteenth-century historians and explorers. Titles include a wealth of travel accounts and diaries, histories of nations from throughout the world, and maps and charts of a world that was still being discovered. Students of the War of American Independence will find fascinating accounts from the British side of conflict.

Social Science

Delve into what it was like to live during the eighteenth century by reading the first-hand accounts of everyday people, including city dwellers and farmers, businessmen and bankers, artisans and merchants, artists and their patrons, politicians and their constituents. Original texts make the American, French, and Industrial revolutions vividly contemporary.

Medicine, Science and Technology

Medical theory and practice of the 1700s developed rapidly, as is evidenced by the extensive collection, which includes descriptions of diseases, their conditions, and treatments. Books on science and technology, agriculture, military technology, natural philosophy, even cookbooks, are all contained here.

Literature and Language

Western literary study flows out of eighteenth-century works by Alexander Pope, Daniel Defoe, Henry Fielding, Frances Burney, Denis Diderot, Johann Gottfried Herder, Johann Wolfgang von Goethe, and others. Experience the birth of the modern novel, or compare the development of language using dictionaries and grammar discourses.

Religion and Philosophy

The Age of Enlightenment profoundly enriched religious and philosophical understanding and continues to influence present-day thinking. Works collected here include masterpieces by David Hume, Immanuel Kant, and Jean-Jacques Rousseau, as well as religious sermons and moral debates on the issues of the day, such as the slave trade. The Age of Reason saw conflict between Protestantism and Catholicism transformed into one between faith and logic -- a debate that continues in the twenty-first century.

Law and Reference

This collection reveals the history of English common law and Empire law in a vastly changing world of British expansion. Dominating the legal field is the *Commentaries of the Law of England* by Sir William Blackstone, which first appeared in 1765. Reference works such as almanacs and catalogues continue to educate us by revealing the day-to-day workings of society.

Fine Arts

The eighteenth-century fascination with Greek and Roman antiquity followed the systematic excavation of the ruins at Pompeii and Herculaneum in southern Italy; and after 1750 a neoclassical style dominated all artistic fields. The titles here trace developments in mostly English-language works on painting, sculpture, architecture, music, theater, and other disciplines. Instructional works on musical instruments, catalogs of art objects, comic operas, and more are also included.

old books. new life.

The BiblioLife Network

This project was made possible in part by the BiblioLife Network (BLN), a project aimed at addressing some of the huge challenges facing book preservationists around the world. The BLN includes libraries, library networks, archives, subject matter experts, online communities and library service providers. We believe every book ever published should be available as a high-quality print reproduction; printed on-demand anywhere in the world. This insures the ongoing accessibility of the content and helps generate sustainable revenue for the libraries and organizations that work to preserve these important materials.

The following book is in the "public domain" and represents an authentic reproduction of the text as printed by the original publisher. While we have attempted to accurately maintain the integrity of the original work, there are sometimes problems with the original work or the micro-film from which the books were digitized. This can result in minor errors in reproduction. Possible imperfections include missing and blurred pages, poor pictures, markings and other reproduction issues beyond our control. Because this work is culturally important, we have made it available as part of our commitment to protecting, preserving, and promoting the world's literature.

GUIDE TO FOLD-OUTS MAPS and OVERSIZED IMAGES

The book you are reading was digitized from microfilm captured over the past thirty to forty years. Years after the creation of the original microfilm, the book was converted to digital files and made available in an online database.

In an online database, page images do not need to conform to the size restrictions found in a printed book. When converting these images back into a printed bound book, the page sizes are standardized in ways that maintain the detail of the original. For large images, such as fold-out maps, the original page image is split into two or more pages

Guidelines used to determine how to split the page image follows:

• Some images are split vertically; large images require vertical and horizontal splits.
• For horizontal splits, the content is split left to right.
• For vertical splits, the content is split from top to bottom.
• For both vertical and horizontal splits, the image is processed from top left to bottom right.

THE

MASQUERADE,

A

P O E M.

INSCRIBED TO

C – – – T H – – D – – G – – R.

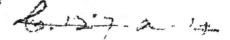

———— *Velut ægri somnia, vanæ*
———— *Species* ———— Hor. Art. Poet.

By LEMUEL GULLIVER,
Poet Laureat to the King of LILLIPUT.

LONDON,
Printed, and sold by J. ROBERTS, in Warwick-lane;
and A. DODD, at the Peacock, without Temple-bar.
MDCCXXVIII.
[Price Six pence.]

THE
DEDICATION.

S I R,

I Believe no one will dispute your right to this little poem, any more than your presiding over that diversion it celebrates, therefore I shall, without excuse, lay it at your feet

The flattery of dedications has been often exploded: to avoid the most distant imputation of which, I shall omit several things that (perhaps) might not be justly so called. and that the more readily, since your merit is so well known, it would be only publishing what is in every one's mouth.

I cannot, however, help congratulating you on that gift of nature, by which you seem so adapted to the post you enjoy. I mean that natural masque, which is too visible a perfection to be insisted on here — and, I am sure, never fails of making an impression on the most indifferent beholder.

Another gift of nature, which you seem to enjoy in no small degree, is that modest confidence supporting you in every act of your life. Certainly, a great blessing! for I always have observed, that brass in the forehead draws gold into the pocket.

As for what mankind call virtues, I shall not compliment you on them. since you are so wise to keep them secret from the world, far be it from me to publish them, especially since they are things which lie out of the way of your calling.

Here I beg leave to contradict two scandalous aspersions, which have been spread against you.

First,

DEDICATION.

First, That you are a b——d.

Secondly, A conjurer.

Whoever has seen you at a m-fq-r-de, cannot believe the first — and you have given several instances at White's, that you are not the other

But what signifies attempting to confute what needs no confutation ? — Besides, you have so great a soul, that you despise all scandal — and live in the world with the same indifference, that people have at a masquerade, where they are not known.

Smile then (if you can smile) on my endeavours, and this little poem, with candour — for which the author desires no more gratuity than a ticket for your next ball, and is,

S I R,

Your most obedient,

From my garret
in Grub-street.

Humble servant,

LEMUEL GULLIVER.

THE
MASQUERADE,
A
P O E M.

OME call Curiosity an evil,
And say 'twas that, by which the devil
With Eve succeeded in his suit,
To taste the dear forbidden fruit
Others (allowing this) yet wou'd
Prove it has done less harm than good
To this (say they) whate'er we know
In arts or sciences, we owe
To this, how justly are attributed
What W—st—n, H—l—y, have exhibited
From this we borrow hopes of greater
Discoveries of madam Nature
Hence is our expectation gain'd,
To see the longitude explain'd
'Tis this which sets the chemist on,
To seek that secret-natur'd stone,
Which the philosophers have told,
When found, turns all things into gold
But being hunted, and not caught,
Oh! sad reverse! turns gold to nought
Britain may hence her knowledge brag
Of Lilliput and Brobdingnag

T his

This paſſion dictated that voyage,
Which will be parallel'd in no age.
'Twas this which furl d my ſwelling ſails,
And bid me truſt uncertain gales ;
Gave me thro' unknown ſeas a lift,
And, ſpight of dangers, made me Swift.
'Tis this which ſends the Britiſh fair
To ſee Italians dance in air.
This crowds alike the repr'ſentation
Of Lun s and Bullen's coronation
By this embolden'd, tim'rous maids
Adventure to the maſquerades.
And, to confeſs the truth,   twas this
Which ſent me there, as well as miſs.
Now for the benefit of thoſe,
Whoſe Curioſity oppoſe,
Or parents ſtrict, or jealous ſpouſes,
(Rogues! who make priſons of their houſes)
The ſequel all its joys unravels,
Plain as th' adventures in my travels.

    The criticks wou'd be apt to bark,
Was I to leave them in the dark
As to my dreſs — Faith! I appear'd
In the ſtrange habit of a bard
My ſhabby coat you might have known
To have been black — tho' now 'twas brown ·
My breeches (old tradition ſays)
Were new in queen Eliza's days,
And to enforce our faith, we're told
They ne'er were worn with weighty gold.
My goat-ſkin-aping wig (I've heard)
Was made of Hudibras's beard,
Its hairs, in quantity and hue,
Declare its ped'gree to be true.
The laurels did my temples grace,
As did a maſque my uglier face
Thus when equipp'd, I call d a chair,
Go, to th' Haymarket theatre.

    O muſe, ſome ſimile indite,
To ſhew the oddneſs of tl e ſight.

                                        As

As in a madman's frantic fkull,
When pale-fac'd Luna is at full,
In wild confufion huddled lies
A heap of incoherencies.
So here in one confufion hurl'd,
Seem all the nations of the world;
Cardinals, quakers, judges dance;
Grim Turks are coy, and nuns advance.
Grave churchmen here at hazard play;
Cinque-ace ten pound — done, quater-tray.
Known prudes there, libertines we find,
Who mafque the face, t' unmafque the mind.
Here, running footmen guzzle tea;
There, milk-maids flafks of Burgundy.
I faw two fhepherdeffes dr-nk
And heard a friar call'd a p-nk.
Loft in amazement as I ftood,
A lady in a velvet hood,
(Her mein St James's feem'd t' explain,
But her affurance — Drury-lane,
Not Hercules was ever bolder)
Came up, and flapp'd me on the fhoulder.
Why how now, poet! pray, how fare
Our friends, who feed on Grub-ftreet air?
For, be affur'd, we all fhall dub
Thy laureat-brow, with name of Scrub.
No man of any fafhion wou'd
Appear a poet in a crowd.
A poet in this age we fhun,
With as much terror as a dun:
Both are receiv'd with equal forrow,
Who wou'd be paid, and who wou'd borrow.
And tho' you never fpeak — we fpy
The craving beggar in your eye.
For poverty's ftill your hoft,
The tim ly   —— ——
Aad us, to will afan, we're giv'n
Th poetry, the road to heav'n.
V hy   (this   )   churchmen fay,
F d   y.
W ll   n,   n)
I m o o ,   n

Tho' in this garb — I'm in reality,
A young, smart, dapper man of quality.
No lawrels — but a smart toupee,
In drawing-rooms, diftinguish me.
I often frisk it to the play,
To Norfolk's, Kemp s and Strafford's day.
An opera I never mifs;
To shew my teeth — I fometimes hifs
I'm feen where-e'er the ladies flock,
My converfation's — What's a clock?
Then of the weather I complain,
No matter whether wind or rain,
Or hot or cold, for in a breath,
I'm fometimes fcorch'd, and froze to death.
Rain has been often the creation
Of a dry frozen converfation.
No wind e'er rages, but it blows
In fympathetic mouths of beaux.
Enough! (the lady cry'd) I fee
You are, indeed, the man for me
For all our wifer part defpife
Thofe little apifh butterflies,
And if the breed been't quickly mended;
Your empire fhortly will be ended:
Breeche, our brawny thighs fhall grace,
(Another Amazonian race)
For when men women turn — why then
May women not be chang'd to men?

    But come, we'll take a turn, and try
What myfteries we can defcry.

    Hold, madam, pray what hideous figure
Advances?   Sir, that's C——t H—d—g—r.
How could it come into his gizzard,
T' invent fo horrible a vizzard?
How could it, fir? (fays fhe) I'll tell you·
It came into his mother s belly,
For you muft know, that horrid phyz is
(*Puris naturalibus*) his vifage
Monftrous! that human nature can
Have form'd fo ftrange burlefque a man

                                        Why,

Why, fir, (fays fhe) there are who doubt
That nature's felf ne'er made it out
For there's a little fcrip which refteth
Of an old regifter, attefteth,
That Amadis being convey'd,
By magic, to th' infernal fhade;
By magic, there begot upon
The fair Tyfiphone, a fon
And that, as Mulciber was driv'n
Headlong, for's uglinefs, from heav'n,
So, for his uglinefs more fell,
Was H—d-- g—r tofs'd out of hell,
And, in return, by Satan made
Firft minifter of 's mafquerade.
Now this his juft preferment bears,
'Mongft wits, the name of Kick-up-ftairs
Madam (fays I) I am inclin'd,
(Tho' of no fuperftitious mind)
To think fome magic art is us'd,
By which our fenfes are abus'd.
For what can here this crowd purfue,
Where they all nothing have to do?
Nothing! why fee at yonder fide-board
What fweetmeats mifs does in her hide hoard.
A little farther take your eye,
And fee how faft the glaffes fly.
Again furvey the inner room,
There trembling gamefters wait their doom.
Here the gay dance the fair employs;
There, Damon fues forbidden joys,
Whilft Sylvia, liftening to his pray'r,
Gives him no reafon to defpair.
See, where poor Doris tries t' affwage
The haughty Laura's fiery rage,
Who caught him with a rival miftrefs,
(The fad occafion of her diftrefs)
For drinking, gaming, dancing — and
Contriving to — you underftand —
(What well-bred fpoufes muft connive at)
Are the chief bus'neffes they drive at.
Some, indeed, hither fends good-nature,
To vent their o'er-grown wit in fatyr.

F

Some

The MASQUERADE.

ome spend their time in repartee,
Others, rare wits, in ribaldry.
Whilst others rally all they see,
With that smart phrase, " Do you know me ? "
Below stairs hungry whores are picking
The bones of wild fowl, and of chicken ;
And into pockets some convey
Provisions for another day,
Preparing thus for future wants,
They've both the sting and care of ants
But see Loretta comes, that common ——
Madam, how from another woman
Do you a strumpet masqu'd distinguish ?
Because that thing, which we, in English,
Do virtue call, is always took
To hold its station in the look
Poet, quoth she, (first having shaken
Her sides with laughter) you're mistaken.
Your brother bards have often sung,
That virtue's seated in the tongue :
With you, nor them can I agree,
For virtue's unconfin'd and free ;
Is neither seated here nor there,
A perfect shadow, light as air,
It rambles loosely, every where.
In miss's heart, at ten it lies ;
At twenty, mounts into her eyes ;
Till forty, how it does dispose
Of its dear self, no mortal knows.
The tongue is then its certain station,
And thence it guards the reputation.
Again (says she) some others ask,
They'll tell you virtue is a masque :
But it wou'd look extremely queer
In any one, to wear it here
Madam (says I) methinks you ramble ;
What need we this your long preamble ?
Well then, as in the different ages,
So virtue in the different stages
Of female life, its station alters :
It in the widow's jointure shelters,

In wives, 'tis not so plain where laid;
But in the virgin's maidenhead.
A maidenhead now never dies,
'Till, like true phœnix, it supplies
Its loss, by leaving us another.
For she's a maid, who is no mother.
And she may be — we see in life,
A mother, who is not a wife
Now 'tis this case, which in the trumpet
Of fame distinguishes a strumpet
This, having been Loretta's fate,
Did to the world her loss relate.
So, poor Celi tho it befel,
With secret injuries, to swell,
But had Diana thro' her clan,
(To try how far th' infection ran)
Forc'd all her followers to tryal
Of chastity, by ordeal;
Who knows (tho' it had rag'd no higher)
What pretty feet had swell'd by fire?

But see that knot of shepherdesses,
And shepherds — well — they're pretty dresses.
Such the Arcadian shepherds were,
When love alone could charm the fair.
Such the Arcadian nymphs, when love
Beauty alone in men could move.
How happy did they sport away,
In fragrant bow'rs, the scorching day,
Or, to the Nightingales soft tune,
Danc'd by the lustre of the moon!
Beauteous the nymphs, the swains sincere,
They knew no jealousy, no fear
Together flock'd, like turtle-doves,
All constant to their plighted loves
How different is now their fate!
Both equally conspire to cheat.
Florus, with lying billet-doux
The charming Rosalind pursues,
Follows her to the play — to court,
Where-ever the beau monde resort

Some half a year he's made that tool,
The wife yclepe a woman's fool.
At laſt the pitying fair relents,
And to his utmoſt wiſh conſents.
No ſooner is the nymph enjoy'd,
Than Florus, fickle youth, is cloy'd.
He leaves her foi another toaſt;
She laughs, and cries— pray—who has loſt ?

　　Madam, ſaid I, a ſimile
Of mine will with your tale agree.
So have I ſeen two gameſters meet,
(Both ignorant that both wou'd cheat)
Throw half an hour of life away,
Cheating by turns in fruitleſs play.
At laſt each other's tricks diſcover,
And wiſely give their throwing over :
At one another laugh, as fools,
And run away to ſeek new culls.

　　Poet, your ſimile is juſt.
But what comes here ? quoth I—a ghoſt ;
I hope the fantom does not ſcare you ?
O no , ſays ſhe　but ſee what's near you
Oh hideous ? what a dreadful face !
Worſe than the maſter's of the place !
Has nature been ſo very ſparing
Of uglineſs, to th' age we are in ;
That our deformity by nature
Art muſt contrive to render greater ?
Quoth ſhe, for different reaſons here,
In different maſques, we all appear,
Some ugly vizards are deſign'd
To raiſe ideas in the mind ;
Which may, like foils, conſpire to grace
The leſſer horrors of the face.
Others in beauteous maſques delight,
To be thought belles for half a night ;
As proud of this ſhort transformation,
As juſtice D——k at c--r--n--t--n.
For know, (tho' 'tis by few believ'd)
Moſt go away from hence deceiv'd :

Error,

Error, (ſtrange goddeſs!) ruleth here,
And from her caſtle in the air,
Carefully watches o'er our motions,
Receives our off'rings and devotions.

Behold, aloft, the goddeſs ſit,
In her appearance a coquette;
Six beaus, as many belles, are ſhown,
On right, and left-hand of her throne.
See Venus, Bacchus, Fortune there;
So, at this diſtance, they appear:
But all are pictures, view them near.
The goddeſs theſe, with ſubtle art,
Has plac'd, to captivate each heart.
For whilſt you with a vain entreaty,
Attack the favourite painted deity,
You fall into an unſeen net;
(By Error on that purpoſe ſet.)
Thus caught, you are oblig'd to wander
Through a myſterious wild meander:
Wearied, at laſt you find the door,
Then hey to wine, or wife or w——re.
Of theſe, no matter which, a doſe
Your ſenſes does in ſleep compoſe;
Waking, all your adventures ſeem
An idle, trifling, feveriſh dream.
This fate, indeed, does not befal
(Tho' much the greater numbers) all:
For ſome o'er-leap with nimble feet;
Others, with ſtronger, break the net:
Then kneeling at the favourite ſhrine,
They make the deity benign.

Now that a g—d may be entreated,
By prayers to images related;
'Twill not be credited by ſome
In England, but by all at Rome.

Thus Fortune ſends the gameſters luck,
Venus her votary a ———
—Miſtreſs—Oh! criticks, ſpare the crime,
Of one who cou'd not find a rhyme.

Bacchus,

Bacchus, that jolly power divine,
To his petitioner fends wine.

The lucky gamefter, when repofe
No longer will his eye-lids clofe,
With triumph feels his loaded breeches,
That bend beneath the weighty riches.
The happy lover, when he awakes,
And a furvey of Celia takes,
As fleeping by his fide fhe lies,
Kiffes, in ecftafy, her eyes,
Her lips, her breaft; devours her charms,
And dies in raptures, in her arms.
The honeft fot, difdaining reft,
Finds joy imperial in his breaft;
As great an emperor as any
In Bedlam, Ruffia, or Germany.

But tho' each godfhip kindly grants
To fome petitioners their wants
Each does refufe (I know not why)
With fome petitions to comply;
And oft requires a hearty prayer,
(Inftead of joys) with woes and care
For view the young unfeafon'd drinker,
Oh L—d! methinks I fmell him ftink here,
Welt'ring, he in his pigfty lies,
And curfes all debaucheries.
The undone gamefter wakes, and tears,
From his ill-fated head, his hairs.
The lover, who has now poffefs'd,
From unknown Flora, his requeft;
(Who with a pretty, modeft grace,
Difcover'd all things but her face)
Pulls off her mafque in am'rous fury,
And finds a gentle nymph of Drury,
Curfes his luft——laments his fate,
And kicks her out of bed too late.
From different fprings, of equal pain,
The gamefter and gallant complain;
The gamefter mourns his lofing lot,
The lover fears—that he has got

These are the scenes—wherein engage
The numbers now upon this stage.
These are the different ends, which all
In different degrees befal.
Now I'll discover who I am :
A muse—Calliope my name.
I stood surpriz'd, whilst from my sight
She vanish'd, in a sudden flight.

FINIS.

Printed in the USA
CPSIA information can be obtained
at www.ICGtesting.com
LVHW061153180724
785791LV00006BA/156

9 781170 430170